Imperfect Fit
Selected Poems

IMPERFECT FIT
Selected Poems

MARTHA KING

WITH AN INTRODUCTION BY
BURT KIMMELMAN

MARSH HAWK PRESS *New York* 2004

Copyright © 2004 by Martha King
Cover art: untitled charcoal drawing, 1984, © Basil King
Book design: Martha King and Tod Thilleman

All rights reserved. No part of this book may be reproduced in any form or by any means, electronic or mechanical, including printing, photocopying, recording, or by any information storage or retrieval system, without permission in writing from the publisher.

First Edition
Printed in the United States by Fidlar Doubleday Inc.

Some of these poems are previously published. Grateful acknowledgement to the editors and publishers of *Brief, Chelsea, Giants Play Well in the Drizzle, House Organ, Monday Through Friday* (Zelot Press, 1987), *New American Writing, Radical Poetics*, and *Sparks of Fire: Blake in a New Age* (North Atlantic Books, 1982). Additional thanks to Claudia Carlson for invaluable technical assistance.

Library of Congress Cataloging-in-Publication Data

King, Martha, 1937–
  Imperfect fit : selected poems / Martha King.— 1st ed.
    p. cm.
  ISBN 0-9724785-1-5
  I. Title.
  PS3561.I4817 I47 2003
  811'.54--dc21   2002153932

Marsh Hawk Press
P.O. Box 206
East Rockaway, NY 11518-0206
www.marshhawkpress.org

☙

imperfect, my beauties
B.   M.L.   H.M.

☙

The Poems

1	65 and Raining
3	Orphé
5	Male myths
8	Husband & Wife
9	A picture of things
10	Bookwork
	in 10 parts
20	Six playing cards
	A history lesson
	The Union Card & Paper Company
	In Waldensia
	Telling the story everyone wants
	Domestic life
	It's that
25	Subjects for poetry in the 20th century
27	Anglo English
28	A story
31	Raleigh Road
33	Shenandoah elegy
34	Variation on a line by Osip Mandelstam
35	How to Recover from the War
	in 13 parts
47	Manassas Battlefield Memorial
50	Kitty Blake
52	Cloister

54   Dead friend, still available

56   Lily Variations
        in 4 parts

60   River in January

61   A Lily Sequence
        Easter
        In June
        In August

63   Two for summer
        By day
        Arriving at Celo

64   Ailanthus songs
        in 5 parts

71   A Valasquez Mirror
73   Dear you, my sense
76   The editor notes
77   M to B
79   Spill

Sympathy for the Mortal: An Introduction

Celebrating imperfection, the actual, indeed the everyday that is turned into poetry, *Imperfect Fit* is the first collection of poems from Martha King in many years—her recent books consist of memoir that may be more of a piece with these poems than with early work (as she writes in "Bookwork," "My name's a mistake if I was loved or not / in 'Martha' the dreadful and dear are one / said my mother's stories"). Yet the poems span a long period of time, and show the emergence of the poet's attention—attending to things that gather the world, as Heidegger would say, into a coalescence. The elegance and grace in these new poems resides in the conflation of classically beautiful tropes and gestures with the commonalties, with even the grittiness, of the moment, then another moment, and another. Time in its integers, in the life lived in its momentary details, is gently though piercingly contemplated. Out of this attention the universal peeks through here and there, but it is the now, the "imperfect fit" of presence, which holds on, which stays with you after the covers of this book are shut. And what fills time is the poet's sympathy for the mortal, the flesh and bone, and the fragile consciousness as it confronts the world. In "A Picture of Things Basil Gives Me" she notes: "dick from his heart, his heart on a pole, / he / grows a tree / and arrives in a hurry."

What most characterizes this book's poetics is artful juxtaposition (as in "River in January" where "shards of ice / scream like birds"), which awakens us to the palpable and at times the painfully exquisite. This strategy is powerfully borne out in King's writing-through a found poem, "How to Recover from the War," taken from *Psychology for the Returning Serviceman* (1945), in which the pain of war colors civilian existence and rouses us to the sacrificial deed and its aftermath by way of odd yet quotidian situations. In the section of the poem titled "Picking Out a Wife" the book/poem advises, "You won't have too much choice / Happily. Happiness / Lack of conflict / Wise, wise / Always bursting into tears. . . ." These poems attest a rich life lived in sumptuous, sinew-and-breath detail—a body of work that stands the test of time.

—BURT KIMMELMAN
June, 2004

65 and Raining

rising in Kyoto

a mist crosses Asia

up there

      where it's tomorrow

the children

gone for the day

rain beads on grass blades, and they

bend with the weight

65, says the radio, light

rain in Melbourne

in San Francisco

it is dark, 66 and clouds

64 in Kuala Lumpur

the mills of war

      stop

a cool swath across the world

the house

is quiet

in her dream she

stops

the red devourer feeding on terror

      is not goaded

drizzle in Bedlam noon

pause in Belfast

    65 and raining
           in North Spain

the miners will rest
out of plastique, out,
almost, of rage
the millers of war
are quiet

        scars ache vaguely—
        New Delhi gutter dogs
        lift their snouts—
        raining and 65

clouds in London
rain is expected
65 in Bucharest
and we
in bed together
hear the radio announce
65 and raining
on the earth

Orphé

the motherless boy loves handling food
stands at my table chopping garlic
showing me how to pulp a clove
with the flat
side of a knife

mincing it
repeating a
restaurant fantasy in a future he won't do

It's a descant
              decant   he can't be sure
needs to handle food—objects of existence
is what he calls the mushrooms
and the lettuce

Later he says, Lawrence is right
women write different

Later he says, he is waiting to be
                              a woman some day
sings
below
in the underworld

mother? Mother?
Was I a little dog once?
Turned out and tamed
lifting my leg at barber poles
wagging my male hindquarters
in my last life?

Male Myths

male myth, unnumbered

wheeling a barrow of hot macadam
dumb as a drone, ox, or mule

all vibration is vibration
even the whistle only dogs hear

big
dumb
bell
forever outside with brothers

•

male myth, persistence

clubs, scattered
cudgels
a burden of hardwood

not what I
remembered

•

his myth

pitted old bronze-painted sword
                a fake
Etruscan who shamed the servers

they took revenge
unhinged the arched chest
crossed his spread legs
and tipped his black-rimmed, staring battle-eyes

hid away, the bloody meet
of hunter and prey
is lied about

•

male myth, another

He dances on vases
He promised a troubled sleep
We don't connect him
        one   to   another
    Lounging in silks
    With a pearl hat on

Poised on a fat horse

If the line here is short or absurdly complex

he is not soon in his great business

Husband & Wife

male & female
says the keeper of the secret
a mathematical principle

the cheap textbook explains
she's wide-hipped
and he's
broad-shouldered
a mogen david centerfold
less to more

to take command
of the situation
is the job of a weaver
o sexual invention
plotting between
poles and coils
                    but husband?
    see my hand?
    my wrists are wrinkled
    & see my wife?
    she lies beside me also

A picture of things
Basil gives me

rocks, pots,
                little eyes on bags of gold
        dinner
                        on a rolling plate
              dick from his heart, his heart on a pole, he
                  grows a tree
  and arrives in a hurry

                                    skiing on one leg
with rings floating around the eyes of a chromium sun

                           and he has opened his mouth to sing!

Bookwork

Book One

You are
destination as well as transportation.
That word is home or boat;
that word is way, or river
that "you", remember? disguised whatever was socially not okay to say
about the person you loved: sex or identifier.

This is modern times
the words "husband" and "householder"
are agricultural
they frame inheritance, with notions of saving and possession,
of land to be occupied, turf to be bossed
       (All mothers are maids,
        the child said.)

She asked, "What do they want from us," passing the subway
prayer fest
a dozen gathered to quaver
     mother, mother
     mother, believe us!
What do they want from us? she said.
No useful word here…
They can see you in dreams as mother of corpses.

You are a road, a way, home and the goal
"You" a word for the one "we" love

I am afraid; I dreamed your death, floundering for road.

What do "they" want from "you"? or from "us"?

Think "conceit" as in literary
look up "honor" and "elegiac": remember we are using language
Remember how language fails us.

Book Two

We sat on square rocks
one person, one rock,
our calves pressed against warmish stone
in an orderly landscape

This is a small story

The sun was not hot and shared the same sky as the moon
we sat in a mildness made partly of car exhaust
soothing as used bath water, familiar as
unclean sand

No obvious signs of distress

Someone trapped the wan light on a photograph negative
and some flat part of then became future now
eighteen months before your illness was evident

No signs of distress
but your day pack was housing

an armamentarium of
>> arnica, lavender,
>> gentian violet
medicinals of Egyptian usage,
aromatics against putrefaction
in with the tampax and sugarless chewing gum

They seemed simply part of your charming absorption
You were always concerned
to be granted good options, to enlist the concern of your parents
and friends, to live in a place of physical beauty
Facile means easy to handle

This story is facile
There were no sensations un-lulled by grey sun
no ideas out of sync with the soiled lake water
>> goes shush lick, shush lick,
>> lick, lick, lick,

Book Three

We sit on square rocks
toes pointing up
calves pressed against stone
we think it's you thinks it's me thinks it's whose

The child draws
stick parades   polygons   sun-shields
the moon sings a Chinese song to the cow
breath soughs over adenoids

No one stops time

But a triskelion speeds down the beach
betting against the event

we think it's you thinks it's me thinks it's whose

The child breaks in two
breaks in two

Book Four

Mother, are you sitting in your mother's chair?
   was this chair chopped for kindling by the vicious Mr. Schiff
   or borne away to Charleston
   by Great Uncle Phil
   mourning the death of his mother, Martha the Poet

My name's a mistake if I was loved or not
in "Martha" the dreadful and dear are one
said my mother's stories

I love grey, Martha said
the grey of stones, the grey of smoke and elegant suede

Grey is also dead faces, dishpan water, the rotting beans are grey
as unwashed sheets, the
      colors of hunger and shock.
Greys are us ofays, as much as greys are the ocean in storm, and

grey the last light each one of us
        sees—the beautiful grey of all mixtures
        the grey E , the gray A
My great grandmother Martha's grey grey hair
the Martha who taunted and killed
        The grey of my name

She gave me these fiery stories: the rages and teeth
chairs chopped to kindling, the fires set, the trapped man who
        burned
shrieking at midnight
day after day her yellow teeth flashed as they rolled over language
books of it, all in her head
Mother, are you sitting in your grandmother's chair?
        in the house sold years ago
            as your slow cigarette smoke curls up through the lamp shade
            as the words in your books turn grey?

Public Books

Book One

How can we bear this inherited shame
Which has happened again

Our shame that ruin
      is possible

The cities have spoiled; knowledge collapsed
Chopped limbs are tossed in trenches
Grotesque trophies flash on computer screens
are hawked in magazines

We grubbed in the ruins without georgics or husbandry
Plagues took us, aqueducts clogged
The sanitary engineers were perished

When the last glasses broke, no one had any more

Then saints taught us purity lies in the heart

We cooked up crude soap in stupid black kettles

People said angels explain it

Book Two

In old books the beautiful and gifted concubine dies young, persecuted
        by her ritual superior and sexual rival
and in the Peony Pavilion the woman returns after death to join her
        lover

Topos

Segregated lives fold close in orthodoxy's arms
Speech depends upon listeners

Once, speech for men was public and the key to self-cultivation
A woman's speech was coded as sexual
        suitable for intimate emotions
        it thus embraced and enclosed

Some rooms are public, even at home
There is seclusion, and there is the sense of being known
There is an invisible door but what good does it do?

Book Three

my flexible treasure's as
common as breakfast

ours is the dominant tongue

more ways to say plenty

more coffee and milk

more easy appropriate
easy
transform
eggs over easy
happily claimed

as native as greed, my cherry, my walnut,

yellow mulberry and yam

Book Four

Paul A loves coincidence too much
Paul B provides a speech on tape
    I pronounce lack of trust in words
Who listens?

Music a silent shower stall
Radio car with windows rolled up
In public books
Long stories duke it out
    as a rundown with check marks and prizes

Tick
ten tales Odyssey down-home in the Delta
intimacy engenders
Tock
Tick

nine memoirs on learning how to live

eight Tock of baffled and beleaguered

seven tales creating

manhood Tick

six domestic chronicles Tock the marriage of five poets

discussing why the universe displays

four irregularities

Tock three essays on what slavery left

Tick two crooked texts tack

one brother Teck

    Tuck

Book Five

       To read

is bookwork too

To hear rocks clink

place ear

on water

thinking without thinking

stream idle

 idyll

  idol

   eidolon

To read but not to see

Book Six

A psychiatrist who wishes to believe
in the redeeming power of art
who wishes he were not frightened of his patients

who writes as honestly as he can about
viet vet post traumatic stressed men
and Achilles' breakdown...
ignores the celebration of evil bloodymindedness
the blatant premise of the Saxon bards

Six Playing Cards

A history lesson

At the back of the store
      or out on the porch
they once played a long game called euchre
sounds like something bad you do to a goat

In fact, no one plays this game now
but it caused the birth of the Joker
who has nothing to do with the Hanged Man, the Fool
   or even the Juggler
     who has nothing to do with Mercury,
       Hermes, or Ariel
Who is related to Coyote,
  West Africa's Spider, or the cannibal Badger of Nippon
only in the hustles of splendid coffee-table books

    Euchre Best Bower!
    all bets are off
    the bee scratches his nuts
    the jockey plays baseball
    and a freelance recluse in Climax, Utah
     is carefully painting a tri-colored cap and bells

Union Card & Paper Company

In this country, Kings wear hats

They sit on brick walls

a vantage for viewing

      baby drunkards holding up their mugs

          Then   corn

                  cupids

            boars

        dogs who smoke pipes

        elephants and snakes

        and ladies, oh the ladies, with so many spicy buttons

                a neat coiled whip

          and a record book

In Waldensia

Put your trust in god, said the juggler
for you cannot even predict on which of six sides
        my dice will land
    you will choose the wrong badge
                and support crimes against your own heart

Power hangs in the balance
            that will not stay
put your trust, he says
             smiling
your combinations flee
gambling is your passionate suspension
even refusing to choose is a choice
and this is Europe, you fool,
    the pigs of your grandfather
    ate this earth

             Dahling, dahling
             put your trust. . .

Telling the story everyone wants

Listing the colors
    one silver birch
    two nails rubbed by shoe soles
    and grays, why not, hundreds of catkins
Now let's go inside

        In here you're perfect

you have money and brains
the things you buy will last forever
of course we're afloat
you know tidal powers are to be expected
you comprehend it completely
I'll tell the colors:
> swimming-pool blue
>
> orange-rind orange
>
> cream with the palest green specks
>
> this languid abundance,
>
> these freckles and dots of *amour*

Domestic life

Jack called Jill a card
and lost his crystal
crawling across the washing machine
to plumb
> —up to his armpit—

the infernal crack behind the pantry wall
reaching for a book
> called chili madness

It's that

tooth of the rhino-saurus
the elephant's horn that won't fit
> in the cardboard bag

it's this war of abstractions:
we know better
we do worse

the green floor shines, while the drains carry away what's refused
we think an orderly calm awaits us, which we wouldn't want if we were
        really
                unhappy
    a decorated simplicity
        a carved abstraction for our pleasure,
            easy to pack and run with
                easy to see

Subjects for poetry in the 20th century

List is mania
collections of images
the personal isn't
why I don't care about your grandmother in the sunset
why I do
the connections between things: yellow flags over and beyond
    national politics, warnings at sea, marsh flowers
conversions between things or from one thing to another thing
    lightning selects only one tent pole
    the pulse changes
seduction and numbness
the essential necessity of confusion
    out of dirt, temporary organization
    her fire gave me goosebumps

But it was more
subjects and poetry
    subjected
        subjective
will it be clearer if you look under the table?

Will you be quiet?
    can quiet
        quiet

Quiet and feel the squares on which we walk, drive;
the circles from which we drink, eat;
the oblongs we handle, raise, read, look out of, open, shut;
the rareness of triangles.

Anglo English

Shackleton, Shadwell
Skeat above Skelton
Whose big green cape quoth Calliope

Get outta my face line pockets line eyelids redline blueline
        mainline infree
line in the supermarket, picket line, movie line, jet lines a skyblue cool as
a baseball seam, line drive a fly streak
flypaper curl
oh sticky brown shoe store in Cleveland, Ohio
shoe-shore, she sells – Outta my face!

That means you, buster,
big mouth
cream of the candy butchers
king a the airplanes
queen a the coupons
Gimme some room for manitoos
for growin' Cambodian doughnut chains

Shackleton, Shadwell
Skeat above Skelton
Whose big green cape quoth Calliope

A story

We came home from the movies
my face aching
with laughter
      and my husband
      turns on the TV
           for a story. . .

           there is the princess
           in a tower
           the man
           who breaks custom
           the fat detective—and the one who's stoned
           the troubador
           's lady
           the bird with strange eyes . . .

The threads tatter
and we're hungry again

      bar jokes
      true confessions
      the night Joe told me
      how his father died —

    even his terror

        is a

        story

    i'm hungry for

            "England is an old house

            stuffed with stories"

            the book began

            Street doors have been altered

            and a building i knew well

            is demolished

                    a tale

            "My grandfather sold his shop,"

            another begins

Even in arithmetic books:

"Jan had three apples"

she needed to

count

the seeds . . .

                        it is no sooner finished

                  than others unroll themselves

        Anyone who'll cry
              "gather round!"
      gets a listener to begin with
only "the end"
is ridiculous

None of us believe it

Raleigh Road

Raleigh, we've not been beyond
earshot of builders for ten generations

in a cloud of noise and dust
huge yellow cats
clamber the red hill
rupturing oak roots

the wheel is visceral, rolling in blood
the grit is orange
        black spots of august
        tannic and diesel fuel
        hot in my face
your road in America

always the personal—
please bring me health!
I read of an old friend's death as if
        this
        road had never been paved

great trees at the verge won't survive
already their green leaves whiten

oh shoulders
> of innocent skin

they build my America, Raleigh
Stop for a pipe and discuss it, my red hungry friend

Shenandoah elegy

People who can't recover from the war
sit on the front porch
saw the chair rockers against the wood floor
and watch the valley's slow tide
        green up
                and die away

Paint on the porch banister fades and peels
Kind hands bring dinner plates
fried yams, pork chops

        The seasons peak and recede across graying fields
        Agitated starlings follow the hay cutters
        It is replaced

People who can't recover from the war
        sit
    for fifty years
  names on a slab or
on the tongue of a grandmother, remembering

A valley famous for the hate of women
      ambiguous as
            the smoky eyes of its gray veterans

Variation on a line by Osip Mandelstam

"There is grass in the streets of St. Petersburg"
it is my childhood and
the last new thing
has already happened

in Amherst
the hedge at the Dickinson house
reaches second story windows

the last new thing
the song goes
sacred belief of childhood
    there is grass

the streets of St. Petersburg buckle
at soft green spears
why is nobody trampling them?
warfare and riots have broken our hearts

no new thing happened
the song goes
sacred belief
we are not the first to promise we'll arrive

    grass   *grass*   *grass*

How to Recover from the War

A found poem extracted from *Psychology for the Returning Serviceman,* prepared by a committee of the National Research Council, and edited by Irvin L. Child, Yale University, and Marjorie van de Water, Science Service. Infantry Journal/Penguin Books, 1945. Twenty-five cents.

Note from the Introduction: Perhaps you will want to keep this book for further use after you have read it. Or perhaps you would prefer to tear out certain chapters for rereading later on.

Out of uniform
Like a rosy dream
From having to do things you hate
Have things changed?
Some have married
Foolish civilian talk
You are likely to be surprised
Be calm. Somehow. How long were you in the asylum?
Problems to face
Mar married happiness
Other jobs, political parties, religious groups, racial or national
       groups, labor or capital
Regrets over your fallen friends
Pull such an idea out it helps
The important to be done
There will be wars to fight after all the guns are silent
Smooth highways. Rough detours
Your way toward that goal

Meeting problems and looking ahead

Cold mud or jungle heat, isolated post, clean bed, a restless

feeling of discontent. You need something deeply

Truly

You need to know what to do about it

What a man wants

Any likely human animal

Rest. Water. Food. Sexual need is another powerful desire

The common needs. Honey, molasses or syrup,

and plenty of butter

Sex needs are also complicated

Conflicting desires

Perhaps Australia. You are still fond

Not so good because you don't like the new people

Making a decision

Write down in the same way

Consider as a possibility:

    1) something you can get today

    2) anything unpleasant which won't occur

Very often, it seems, when you buy something on the installment plan

or when you borrow money and give your note

you have avoided getting

in debt by putting it off

Why you worry

Because it is just as impossible to turn yellow as it is to forget

So men often think

I can't stand the way these women talk

It takes effort

Powerful opponent blocks you, what do you do?

Hard jobs. Long work results in failure, and this happens a number of times

Fail on the examination. Tear it up. Take it out on the cheap and hunting for trouble. Sober or drunk a man may even commit suicide

Finding a new objective

Possible to satisfy, perhaps, small son at Christmas

Decide to be a pharmacist or a physical training instructor

Daydreams and talk

Later on

can be a sign that you'd

rather talk than act

Abandoning objectives

Apathetic, cold, unresponsive, they refuse

Such men are men who have failed, failed time after time

After success

If you are like most

Throw yourself into struggle

Prisoner of War

No, the Whites shut down that gasoline station years ago

Ed White went to work in the munitions factory and his boy didn't even wait until he was 18. Joined the Marines when he was 17 and did right well, too. The old man ran the place for a while, but then his health failed and he had to give it up—didn't have much to sell anyway

If you have been a prisoner

When you were a prisoner

Were bad. Extreme. But under humiliation, the confinement, the hard life is not able to hurt them so much

Barbed wire

Inner defenses

In the first place

It isn't his fault

A nurse, a WAC, or civilian women of the area

Hard to forget the obscene talk that becomes commonplace

From the first minute

Ways of passing time

Being dependent for everything you got to eat and wear and for candy,
                                  books, playing cards

Nerves

on edge

Gripped by the warm and comfortable

Sensitive to loud noises

Sunlight disagreeable

Full diet also to steady your nerves

Plenty of other things happen to you

All this built up in you a great deal of tension

Harried, restless, and sometimes bitter

"Barbed Wire Disease"

But you have already made a difficult adjustment from the life of a combat soldier or sailor to life as a P.O.W.

You got along

Getting well

To kill is a soldier's main job

And yet when you drive your bayonet into the flesh of a man, it may seem a terrible thing to you

Some men never forget it

The bombardier

who spills his deadly load from three or four miles up

may not feel

this

If you feel bad about having been a killer, and dream

They hated to kill

They hated war

Your own good sense may tell you that there never was

at any time

anything you could do to prevent it.

This is not an unusual cause of combat nerves

Getting away from battle made you worse

One of your troubles is

until you get used to noise

juke joints won't help you any

Don't take a job in a boiler factory

You can wear dark glasses and earplugs for a while

For many the morning after more than balances

the good it does when you drink

Don't try to rush things

A year, two years, even longer

You may be urged by friends or relatives

Battle has left you shaking

Feel your way

On a job considerably below your abilities

Work out some way to live away from home

Going over and over your thoughts isn't good for you

You are going to run into other men who have combat nerves

People are going to say silly things

Go to bed at night too tired to dream

Develop the ability to see your problems

      as a man from Mars

Look back. Humor helps

Don't do it except to the right person

psychiatrist, psychoanalyst

Others have a good deal of understanding

Bad listeners are likely to be too sympathetic

shocked, worried

give too much advice

You need to be able to distinguish

Yesterday, today, and tomorrow

have a way of merging

As soon as you have heard the sound of the gun, its shell

can never reach you

Gone

Your mental health is all right again

Choosing a job

Similar kind. Some facts. Chances.

Skills

1, 2, 3, 4

because of changes in industrial methods, use of substitute materials, and so on. Judgments about aptitude

1, 2, 3, 4. Tests.

Interests

degree, consider, leave

Tests of Interests

wiring/ clients/ speech/ soldiers/ horses/ reports

You may enjoy working with women, or you may hate it

Second Choices

Even a bad job

Learning new skills

Greek or mathematics

A new city

What learning is

Cars, for example

Essential action

You sell a car

Things go wrong

Skill in trying out these things mentally, many skills,

The simplest and easiest kind is the tying up of a natural inborn way

Let in the clutch

Nature should be reduced

It does not mean, however, that thought is unnecessary while you are learning. Thinking helps at the learning stage.

>
> What Hinders Learning
> Emotion Can Help
> Be Eager To Learn
> Do It Yourself
> Don't Learn Mistakes
> Profit From Demonstrations
> Make Use Of Words
> Take Rest Periods
> Get An Over-All View
> Don't Be Discouraged By Temporary Lack Of Progress

Getting married

Why men marry:

He wants the buttons sewn on his shirts

An outlet for powerful sex drives, that won't get him talked about

That is safe from disease, that is respectable

A man may marry a charming woman

in somewhat the same spirit that he

picks out a good car or builds a nice house

A wife is sometimes the ideal person to tell things to

Important to a man's standing in the eyes of his employer

Good reason

Not so likely to take chances, to leave looking for change or adventure

Entertain friends and acquaintances

Love

Because she is the one person who can best satisfy some of his

Other reasons

These are all good reasons for marriage

What are these cravings?

For everything that you have associated with good women since you were born

Rip, smash, crush and hate

Grow, protect and to love

War offers many men plenty of chances to blow things sky high

There is also building in war

And the need is not one simple urge—it means the end of running around, of uncertainty and change

Children

Your hope among mortal beings

Why men don't marry

Not every soldier immediately finds the right girl

Sure of being a good husband

Other girls, worse than any you knew at home, a cheapening of all women

Other kinds of satisfactions, masturbation, attachments with other men

If you liked girls before you went away, you will probably find them attractive when you get back

American girls are more independent

Much better not to give orders to them. Don't tell them where they can't go, who they can't see, how they have to dress or—and this may be extremely important—that they must not work

Still women in overalls and slacks

Better to woo her

Moonlight and kisses are still big

Stand up when she comes into the room

You aren't as well trained in the softer, tender

Shed, death, pain

You have missed something

If you have lost respect for human life

Picking out a wife

You won't have too much choice

Happily. Happiness

Lack of conflict

Wise, wise

Always bursting into tears

If you marry a girl who has had the wrong kind of start in life

Questions about marriage

You didn't inherit your nervous breakdown

Courtship

Moonlight is more fun than sunlight in making love

Good plain

Day

Light

Wrong

"Years of your life"

Given up best years

War experience

For most men

Gains in it

Many practical tests of battle

Courage, endurance, and true friendship

Discomfort, grief, bloodshed

Some men are made bitter

No one gives a damn

When you came up against the real thing you knew better

You will always realize

Hungry, cold, sick, so tired they can hardly stand

More of a man than you were before

Up to you

In the service

In this sense

Understanding

One way you can take

"Best years of your life"

Manassas Battlefield Memorial

Caution. Please use care.
Driving tours require
turning on and off
heavily traveled
highways.

—National Park Service folder

If there were craters in the fields
they've been smoothed away
but birds who ate wild cedar berries
& sat on fence posts to shit
planted cedar trees
that mark a long-gone fence line

Cars cram the road
turning off and on
& convenient sanijohns are marked
Manassas Battlefield Memorial

Caution, please
this is ground where hunting relics is forbidden

Please use care
save this
for others who come after you

In the heat
the heavily traveled hills
are dim

We can't hear your orders
but you are all around here still
your bleeding feet sopped into the grasses
where you ran
spending yourselves at anyone's command

You came so far, you
were not used with care, packed
into stifling train cars; the hills were dim

Picnickers with wide wicker baskets
crammed the road
to watch the evening news
      (though many ladies grew upset
      and begged their beaux to take them home
the heavily traveled
highways
swollen

      Now, under a young maple
      a general sits
      in a brown field cap & very sleek dark glasses
      long lunch break out of Arlington

      I watch him as he
      stares across the road
      checking errors, instant replay
      (he spends at anyone's command

      Does it interest him
      how your noise reached Washington
      as muffled as explosions over television?

            Under our picnic table
            quick beetles mob the shreds of tunafish and ham

Caution, please
we've come so far

            This road is packed with tourists
            who toss frisbees & forget to throw their trash away
            who stare at monuments and signposts
            and watch the evening's news
            spending us at anyone's command

Kitty Blake

I only know what's not said about you
    Had you
    the bluff rapacious hardiness
    of an English milkmaid?
    big face
    with freckles?

For certain I know you talked a lot
    It was not sheltered for you
    nor did you give false shelter
    your nakedness
    announced everywhere
    in William's specters
        undefended flesh
    quickly labeled
    "mad thing"
    by your neighbors

        Clear the light in the marrow of bones
        though he painted so badly
        soft as the force of a river of light
        impossible to stop
            mending the socks (talking
            stirring the soup (talking

    hearing the rain drip through
            the copper gutters
                    (talking, talking)

A ridged current far below
the milk-white lake top
racing for the spillway

Cloister

for Pete Dandridge

Espalier swollen with hard green pears.
The basement chamber jamming incredible objects my cousin restored.
We see small spots on ivory. Glimmer of chased silver. Folded wood.
Thin animal skin.
The brilliance of melted minerals.

Family romance is a charm to ward off evil spirits.
Sees, as a painted eye on the ship's prow or stares out of blue windows
       as the eyes of Isabella hovered over the dining room table.
The charm rouses riddance, aversion, is a mask of anger.
Entangles intruders who can't find the rules.
Protects through disaster.

This is a dead chamber of intricacy.
We are lured to marvel.
Outside…water ticks on stone.
The construct is an artifice raised to gild a family's romance.
The edifice is real stone.

In the same spirit, we shall pretend the river marks the edge of safety.
The stained cliff holding back
the black wall of wilderness beyond the river.
Literal palisade, provoking fear.

Stone ticks on or is it leaves?
The flat river continues to demonstrate capacity to absorb.
Simply water.
Not endless.

One member of the wealthy family remembers being downstairs
in his nightclothes
to steal a late-night look at their unicorn, the thousand flowers, the stitched mystery of violent death,
the magic rose.

It was never a church.
And so we can examine all that happens here, like students in a laboratory, sneaking a finger onto the old wood, breathing gently against the painted clay, carrying rolls of images home
for the blessing of imagination.

A scene of savage looting. Our glory too.

In such artifacts are narratives. The miniature. The gigantic.
The found and collected.
The spanning.
Not endless, exactly.
        But like rain.

Dead friend, still available...

for Louise Ault

saying so little
you present
the white back of your lover
an april morning, not really warm
bath water in a tub outside

      what could I have done to please him, you still ask
          gleaming and pale
      his back fills the canvas
              water slopes across it, gleaming, pale
      I could not speak about my life with him
        his back fills the view

at his neck, boils and pits
thick poisons rope his muscles, clog his veins
he offers his neck tenderly
trusting in that moment
the weak light, your calm hands

      I did so little
      he said I was too ladylike in bed
      we never spoke about it

      the
      white backs of rabbits in winter
      are almost invisible
      we saw their marks on the cold hills

steaming kettles of skin glue
for his canvases, everything
measured, saved, reversed for even wear
      coffee grounds dug into the vegetable garden
      can reused for brushes, the lid for a floor patch

you saved the furniture, the documents
holding still the cold smell of mean dirt
you held it all
presenting even now
chance staked on a white back, bowing under your hands

Lily Variations
Brooklyn Botanic Gardens

One

a sequence of four
water lily ponds

                in each square
                circles of pads
                the old green shade
                of dollar bills

                there: a half moon
                there: a pale
                reflection of your cheek

                perfect waxy prongs
                flower out of cool underworld

                white fingernails
                    white fisherman
                        male flower harboring
                golden baby in it

Two

Something's in the greenish dark
We want to hear it speak
We want to say we have heard
        Reach out and wet our cheeks with water
                Sniff the scentless
form

Everyone speaks of their excursions
It's not polite
      to call them conquests anymore

                day   light   laves
                  the pads
              air is rising

              white absence of response
              above unmoving oil water

Three

Remember Monet at Giverny
carrying easel and paintbox up the hill
past the geometrical splendor of his cosmos daisies
their army heads dancing
                              in the yellow light?

Remember he is leaving
                        his pond below?

      In the morning, élan vital will rise
      and steam on the pond lid like smoke

                    lily still, lily waiting
                    fish
                            vegetable
                                          lily
                    lotus hermaphrodite
                    cupped on a reflection of itself
                    a cultivated organ
                    throbs dumb words

                    glowing revelations
                    it was bred to indicate

                          perfect prongs
                          pollen baby
                          equally a model
                          of corruption and serenity

Four

Boxes under ice
the twist of bald root
      clear to the bottom
A kid whaps at the ice with a stick
can't stir
the golden carp stuck there

            The summer ponds are all invention
            a tamed picture of the underworld

            A magic trick

            No less accurate than
               peep-hole Easter eggs
                  terrariums
                     or the jungle Rousseau painted
                       in the living room.

River in January

        & shards of ice
           scream like birds

This water used to
seep
glossy & idle
stinking of warm algae & tanker waste

Now
the whole kitchen staff's gone nuts
      clashing pots!   dumping silverware!

While
relentless water engine
is hauling ice hunks
row   after   row

A Lily Sequence

Easter

    As if flowers were ikons of virginity and death
    their scent floors the old churches
    till no one who breathes
    believes

In June

    Plain seeker tubes
    a cup of dreams grows everywhere
    The New York Times reports a woman
    who has planted two hundred kinds
    in her half-acre yard

        just lately, she's acquired seven more
        wonders, the report says,
        "where to put them"

        a pure conceit
        as no one imagines she'll hoard them in a drawer

    Below her window   above her yard
    two hundred kinds of bobbing lily, steep throats glowing
    spent blooms dangling at their necks
    two hundred stubborn systems
                    encroaching everywhere

In August

        The bending blades stripe yellow and burn out
        the leftover stalks bend out, weighted at the tip
               nothing is there to hold them
               nothing but the scars
               of dropped blooms

               Lure that keeps us here

               Lure that calls us back

Vegetable dream, the deep striped base of a gone blossom
where stamen and pistol once arched like dancers

They are not, were not silk, or personable, or all that lovely
               lures then
               holding us

               A lure

Two for summer

By day

   the field is full
                  of swallows
by night
            fire flies

  For *us*! the
children say
              holding their small
                   gen
                       itals

Arriving at Celo

how like our car to have driven all that way
parked in the yard, we admire the squashed bugs
   all the dusk
They are Adirondack chairs and hold our drinks on
convenient arm rests
The road still hot but no longer
angry
        says squish me
        into the shapes I'm used to

Ailanthus songs

1

It is
you know the one
the city tree that no one plants

big weed
stink tree
tree of heaven

2

Catalog of attributes

their speed, persistence, vigor
their sudden death

leafing last in spring
in autumn dropping first
      long yellow leaf spines
       clogging gutters

their spongy wood and soft core
their blossoms, green on green
their blossoms, summer long, yellow green, or red

their elegance; their shade
their opulence
the fronds of paradise

their seedlings that sprout like beans
their love of verges, fences, edge land
their delicacy, their
magnificence
         they gnarl like walnut trees, exceed
arms' breadth
tower four stories

        they climb out of gratings
        root in a single rotted brick

their stink

their reek, married to cat piss
        in dank backyards three-quarters dark

the sneezing and swelling they cause

their smell periods, a
drift of peanut butter as sweet leaftips uncurl
        honey with an itch
and then their blooming stench
bitter as uncleaned elevator shafts

known—to botanists—for
supporting imagoes of
a silkwhite butterfly
        those lazy helixes that court in vacant lots
        feed on them only

weed tree rampant

on a field of airshafts

poverty tree

claimer of waste

3

Facts

ailanthus altissima
may reach 90 feet
is male or is female
both blossom, but males drop their blooms
they ripen on females
becoming reddish green
becoming seed keys shaped like small propellers
any time from July to mid-October

ailanthus altissima
tolerant of shade and
acid soils, tolerant of
dryness
            loves the sun
and grows easily 45 feet in 20 years
in good conditions

ailanthus altissima
with the largest compound leaf in nature
up to 30 oval leaflets on a single structure
    "Heavily manured and cut back to the ground each year
        an ailanthus will throw up monster leaves,
            an exciting ingredient in a shrub border" an
English garden book advises
It is the male that smells

       ailanthus was the breath of the Spice Islands
       the reek of mystery East floating out to sea
       transfixing ships of restless Europeans

       the name *ailanthus* a Moluccan word for sky
       very tall, altissima, they said
       meaning tree
       of heaven

4

The story

they are not primitive

they are not weeds

they are not hated

they are not invincible

       two sexes, with fruits and flowers: all
       late refinements in the botanical move
       from ferns to modern trees

       they reached the West a second time

smuggled out of China by Pierre
d'Incarville, Society of Jesus,
agent of Bernard de Jussieu,
charged by him with a secret mission

trees for the cold impoverished West
for the Royal Gardens of Paris
      weeping willow (for romance)
      japonica (for beauty)
      ailanthus and cedrela, now called *toon*
      which lines the streets of Paris
      (for cigarbox wood – and style!)

ailanthus is the third long-lost tree returned to Europe
in modern times
the peach and almond were returned by ancient hands
the list includes

"Chinese" juniper, magnolia, sweet gum,
dogwood, silktrees
giant sequoia,
white pine, and scarlet oak

all living in Asia or America
but lost to Europe in the Tertiary Ice Age
that drove warm loving trees against
Alps and Pyrenees
      which blocked a south retreat

could die of cold again

5

Love song

ailanthus altissima
showing in winter
twigs simple as a crayon drawing

> *don't mistake me*
> *don't mistake me*
> *I only rub my branches*

sky tree
the pest
lover of broken spaces
returner after ground rape
without distinction patching
the city green, holding us
in webs so easily
broken
seeding and stinking

> *don't mistake me*

known for speed, persistence, vigor

and for sudden death

A Velasquez Mirror

On a table 4 fish, 2 eggs, a chili and 2 broken bulbs of garlic
It is a mirror, a painting
What does she see?
She sees she is excluded
I once looked as tearful and resentful; ears folded forward,
sensual lips and firm cheeks;
              consigned to mashing garlic, my arm pierced by the
              scolding finger that urges attention to my station
They wait, beautiful and neglected, the 4 fish (slimy), the 2 eggs (cool)
There is black wine in the shadowy jug
                      Don't get mystical on me

What is in the background is a painting
      a reflection
There is sound there
Two women speak questions
A man's voice replies
These voices are painted
These dresses curl as brush strokes can, moving ridges of light, swift as
      letters
But the garlic-masher's clothing is not like that
She, like me, wears the representation of reality
Her tears reek of garlic

Tending always to description
I perceive the objects in order
first fish, then eggs; first yolks, then albumin

One can glory in the detail of it

the glossy
the delectable
one can; I can;
I, tending always to descriptions
not how it got there
but what it is
I count now 4, 2, 1, 2, 2, 2
the circular story that confirms
how I am here also

1.

Dear you, my sense,
it's foolish to count five

The kinesthetic sense is how you know
the elevator's falling
      where your head is when you wake
the sense of dreams
the sense of dread

      We think a bio-
      logic clock counts the life of cells?

      You, love, with ESP no odder than experience of lies,
      a sense for sure

2.

To John Donne, thought
was an experience "which
      modified his sensibility"

Eliot feared "dis-
      association of sensibility—aggravated by Milton and
          Dryden—from which
                    we have never recovered"

3.

Dear you, my sense,
count how you know
      where your head is when you wake

      you forestall subtraction
      division and shift
      become your senses

            The quality of being sensible
                  taste

The stream from foolish to unconscious
hear

thinking
closure's artifice

4.

So dark on the cold mud road
a music in the landscape
I could not be sure my eyes were open
or that an ordinary world persisted

Knowing with banana-peel fatality
drama comes to terms
that my bare foot is sinking
this is mediation
in a pile of dog shit
not catharsis

The editor notes

There are going to be more of them
        (just get your mitts off)
they are growing like the nightmare maggots you can't stamp fast enough
relentless
implacable
        and, your intellect, of all things, announces sententiously:
                life is this
                big mix, don't run. . .

There are going to be more of them
growing like the fine grass in May
        blow softly   use your mitts
seeker,   tender,   provoker

M to B

"And perhaps Titian will say a few words to me as he steps
into his gondola," said Degas. Paintings wait:
next to me is a man accompanied by
presences; they move tissue light; they speak.
He too speaks to others
and thinks every day, "we are tradition itself,"
          by dint of the practice

     He
drew many lines
then removed their suggestion
again listening to the soft rustle of dresses on stairs? again the stroking
     of bristles? the hum of chests endlessly taking in
and releasing?

     Are you interested in disquisitions on the nature of prayer?
A machine can show you your heart's colors
intricate as Klee's watercolors, as we suspected;
          saints don't guide us, we knew this as
well
else how did we get onto this minefield to start with?

     Is it the dint of a saint's shoes heating a snow print?
No, it's the touch of hand
the egg-shaped glow of a forehead
the push of a single acid-green triangle
trains belch behind the new women
of the nineteenth century; the boat planks so soft
with slime they plunk like sodden velvet; and around the edge
of the lace is a ridge of dried titanium white: he left it there

joyous

as the soft side of a cow or that animal whose colored
dots can be felt by the blind—because they rise, stiff like
old Jack Ho, legacy of an earlier time

It is not just the gondola, but the water that bears it up.

"We are tradition itself," I'm repeating.

This is a greeting from me
                                      on your fifty-third birthday
not just a present sweep I'm using
to keep sorrow back
but a clear ring of words you might speak
as you step up onto the street

Spill

Harsh feathers of water fan a hot road
the straining list of desires
of course I repeat, turning across the wide room where the
same
elements appear again and again, stroking the same shapes
into
aspects
known to me by their imperfect fit
known by me, I jam them into categories

Water has stained the pink road brown
the road in turn forced a
sizzle of ozone an instant aerosol
pink as a burnt match, brown as
coal glowing
      it is the interruptions that are remembered
disjunctions where energy fizzes, inexpert, straining

The feathers fan, a longing across wide spaces, they move so
little, but the air rushes obedient and cradle-like
where the unexpected is real

Photograph by Dave Gearey

MARTHA KING was born Martha Winston Davis in Charlottesville, Virginia, in 1937. She attended Black Mountain College briefly as a teenager in the 1950s, and married the painter Basil King in San Francisco in 1958. She began writing regularly in the early 1970s, after the birth of their daughters, Mallory and Hetty.

Mrs. King edited the eight-page zine, *Giants Play Well in the Drizzle,* which she sent gratis to interested readers from 1983 to 1993. She also briefly produced *Northern Lights International Poetry/Brooklyn Series* and *SpotS* poetry chaplets. She worked in mainstream book publishing in the early 1970s, for nonprofit literary organizations, most notably Poets & Writers, in the late 1970s, and since that time as an editor and writer for voluntary health organizations. Mrs. King is currently director of publications for the National Multiple Sclerosis Society.

Her prose, poetry, and essays have appeared in many small press magazines. Her books are:

Women and Children First, 2+2 Press, 1975
Weather, New Rivers Press, 1978
Islamic Miniature, Lee/Lucas Press 1979
Monday Through Friday, Zelot Press, 1982
Seventeen Walking Sticks, Stop Press, 1997
Little Tales of Family and War, Spuyten Duyvil, 2000
Separate Parts: Six Memory Pieces, Avec, 2002